CW00850707

*Dedicated to our ancestors whose indomitable spirit, faith and fortitude, gave them strength, courage and hope to endure the hardships and afflictions perpetrated by evil men.*

*And to our present generation and generations unborn, who must at all cost and with all determination make sure...Never Again.*

*Lest We Forget*

# Black Codes in Georgia

Published by
The APEX Museum
135 Auburn Avenue
Atlanta, GA 30303

"Where every month is Black History Month®"

ISBN 1-4404-9526-2
9 781440 495267

www.apexmuseum.org

# Black Codes in Georgia

## Table of Contents

# Acknowledgements

We gratefully acknowledge the assistance of Cassandra Pryor, Neetta Black, Jean Carne, Ariel Howard, Candace Skinner and Estella Moore in research and development of this project.

# Person of Color

*1866*...An act to define the term, "persons of color," and to declare the rights of such persons, that all negroes, mulattoes, mustizoes, and their descendants, having 1/8 negro or African blood in their veins, shall be known in this State as, "person            of            color"

# Introduction
# By Alton Hornsby Jr.

*After the English colonies were settled in North America, beginning in the early 17th century, Western European notions of race and ethnicity quickly appeared in the relationships between Native Americans (Indians) and the Euro-American colonists. Racial categorizations generally followed a model of three distinct groups, Caucasoid (or white), Negroid (or black) and Oriental (yellow or some version thereof). Of the three groups, Negroid , because of blacker skin, which was equated with darkness, ignorance, and evil, was on the lowest rung with Caucasoid, equated with light, purity and good, was on top. The Native Americans (red men) were considered just below the Orientals and just above the Negroes. Hence, they were deemed primitive and inferior, but unlike blacks, sometimes noble.*

*Shortly after the first Africans landed from Africa into the American colonies around 1620, American Negro slavery replaced indentured servitude as their principal status of the blacks. The Massachusetts and Virginia colonies took the lead in defining perpetual servitude for Africans and those of African descent based upon the status of the mother. Children born of free mothers, mostly Caucasian, were deemed free; children born of slave mothers (mostly Black) were slaves—consigned to perpetual bondage.*

*The early Slave Codes denied bondspersons all of the rights normally associated with human freedom. Indeed, they were not persons at all, but chattel—property of their enslavers. However, when it came to the adoption of the United States Constitution, following the American war for Independence, in 1787, a compromise was reached between the northern and southern states that allowed bondspersons to be considered three-fifths of a man for purposes of representation and taxation. Nevertheless, in practice, Blacks did not have three-fifths of citizenship rights and as the U. S. Supreme Court confirmed in the Dred Scott decision of 1857 they were not citizens under the U. S. Constitution and had "no rights which any white man was bound to respect."*

*Those Blacks who attained a free status, either through the status of their mothers, manumission, purchase or escape to the North, were free in name only. Scholars have described their status more accurately as quasi free. They were conscripted in almost every aspect of their lives—(free only in their possession of a "freedom pass", indicating that they were not in bondage), and in their abilities to form independent institutions, including places of worship. These laws that segregated and discriminated against "free persons of color" were generally called Black Codes.*

*After the emancipation of the bondspersons at the close of the Civil War in 1865, a period of fluidity existed in the South in the area of race relations. While de facto, that is in practice, there were patterns of segregation and discrimination, particularly in employment and social relations; it was not until the 1880s that these practices were codified into law. A particularly new feature of the laws was the segregation of blacks on railroads and streetcars and their denial of the right to vote and hold office. These new laws, which subsequently were encompassed under the term "Jim Crow", based on a popular minstrel character of the times, in many places, came to be known as Black Codes.*

*Thus, from the post-emancipation period at the close of the 19<sup>th</sup> century until the middle of the last century, African Americans experienced a New Slavery" in the form of the legal and extra-legal caste system under the Black Codes.*

*Alton Hornsby, Jr. Ph.D.*
*Fuller E. Callaway Professor of History at Morehouse College*
*Former editor of Journal of Negro History (25 years)*

vi

# Forward
## By Dr. Akinyele Umoja

*The book Black Codes in Georgia provides the outline of the legal components of white supremacy in the state of Georgia. Mob violence is the aspect of white supremacist terror that becomes the most visual representation in our contemporary memory. While mob violence and lynching were common occurrences, particularly during the Nadir period (years after Reconstruction until the early 1920s) of the Africana experience in the United States, prior to the Civil Rights Movement of the 1960s, racist laws reinforced white supremacist customs and practices that day-to-day institutionalized Black oppression.*

*This book links the slave codes (including limitations for "free Blacks" during Georgia's colonial, pre-Civil War, and Confederate periods), with Black codes to restrict Black progress during Reconstruction, and the "Jim Crow" of the dejure segregation of the state. Presented together one can link Georgia's official and overt white supremacist heritage. Contemporary racial politics in the state can't be comprehended without exploring Georgia's policies of Black oppression. The effects of over two centuries of legal suppression of people of African descent in Georgia can't and haven't been overturned in the state. Racial inequities persist in education, incomes, criminal justice and other indicators of quality of life in the state and throughout the United States. The psychological, social and* economic impact of over two hundred years of white supremacist laws and denial of human rights of people of African descent in the state can not be denied. On the other hand, policy-makers, corporate leaders and average citizens participate in collective denial by refusing to recognize the responsibility that Georgia and the United States' possesses for slavery, segregation and legal oppression.

As a student of the Africana experience in Georgia and the United States south, *Black Codes in Georgia* will make a tremendous contribution to our understanding of the challenges to Black life in Georgia. Along with Michael Thurmond's *Freedom*, Donald Grant's *The Way it Was in the South* and Alton Hornsby's *Southerners, Too?: Essays on the Black South, 1733-1990* should be required text for Georgia's educators and policy makers in developing an appreciation for the struggle of Black Georgians for human dignity and as a basis to change remaining social ills and injustice in our contemporary reality.

*Akinyele Umoja,*
*Associate Professor*
*African-American Studies*
*Georgia State University*

# Overview
## By Michele Mitchell

*Contrary to popular belief, Black Codes did not begin in 1865 in order to govern and restrict the lives of newly freed slaves. In the state of Georgia, you will find that Black Codes were written as early as the 1700's.*

*Whether they were referred to as Slave Codes (pre 1865), Black Codes, or Jim Crow Laws (1876-1967), Black Codes were and are a comprehensive and systematically arranged body of law created to devalue, dehumanize, degrade, disenfranchise, restrict, deny, separate, punish and oppress people of African descent.*

*This system of law was developed to keep from an entire race of people, the privileges and basic human rights afforded to Whites in this State, as well as this country. These laws affected nearly all aspects of Black life, stifling the growth of an entire race of people.*

*Black Codes were not just for those who were enslaved; these laws were enacted to govern the lives of all people of African descent, free and enslaved.*

*Many of the laws that targeted free Blacks in Georgia were so drastic that they even denied free Blacks the opportunity to live in this state, or made it nearly impossible for them to become a resident.*

*Even though Blacks in Georgia could gain their freedom through manumission (to legally emancipate), they were still governed by the* same laws that governed those who were enslaved.

Although free, Blacks in this state were never granted the privilege of citizenship until well after slavery's official end. Though the 14$^{th}$ Amendment of the United States was proposed to Georgia Legislature in 1866, the amendment was not ratified by Georgia until 1868, after first rejecting it in 1866.

his system of law, created in the state of Georgia, had a devastating effect on generations of African descendants that can still be seen in the disparities in housing, employment, salaries, education, the justice system, and the family structure that slavery tore apart.

Blacks are still trying to close the gap created by the "head-start" that the laws of this state afforded whites.

There are over 200 laws included in this book; however, this is just a fraction of the amount that existed in Georgia's Official Code. This book will enlighten readers not only to "the problem of the color line" in our past, but to the conditions that exist today, in order to make a better tomorrow for our children.

# Definition from the Revised Code of Georgia 1863

**Who Are Citizens** -_All free white persons born in this State, or any other State of this Union, who are, or may become residents of this State, with the intention of remaining therein; all free white persons naturalized under the laws of the Confederate States

**Who is White** - Persons having one-eighth, or more, of negro or African blood in their veins, are not white persons in the meaning of this Code

**Status of a mother fixes that of the children** - The status of every person in this State, upon the question of freedom, is determined by the status of his or her mother.

**Free Negroes** - Negroes once slaves who have with their owner's consent left this State to reside in a State or county where slavery is not tolerated, to become free, and free negroes who have changed their residence to any State are within the provisions of this chapter and cannot return hither.

**Article I.** **Who are persons of color** - All negroes, mulattoes, mestizoes, and their *descendants, having one-eights negro or African blood in their veins, shall be known in this state as persons of color.*

*Child legitimate-* when every colored child born before the 9th day of March, 1866, is hereby declared to be the legitimate child of his mother; but such child is the legitimate child of his colored father only when born within what was regarded as a state of wedlock, or when the parents were living together as husband and wife.

*Definition of slaves* -A slave is one over whose person, liberty, labor and property another has legal control.

*Presumption of slavery* -_All Negroes and mulattoes are deemed, and are hereby declared to be "prima facie" slaves, and it rests upon those alleging freedom to prove it

*Mulatto* -A mulatto is one in whose veins there is at least one-eighth of Negro blood

*Chattels* -All slaves are chattels personal, and to be governed by the same laws, accept in cases expressly provided by statute, or where the nature of the property requires a modification of the ordinary rule.

*Natural rights* -The laws of nature guarantee to every man the right to his life and his limbs, unless forfeited for crime. The state of slavery debars no one of this right.

*Dominion of third persons* -While the slave is in the dominion of his master, third persons have no right of dominion over him, farther than the laws that give such right for police purposes.

*Acquisition of slaves* -A slave cannot acquire or hold property. All his acquisitions belong to his master. Gifts to him accompanied by delivery accrue to the benefit of the master; without delivery they cannot be enforced by law.

*Property of slave* -All property held by a slave, with the consent of the master, is subject to the will of the master at anytime.

*Article II. Children follow the mother* - The children of all female slaves shall follow the condition of their mother, and shall belong to the person holding title to the mother at the time of their birth.

*Who are free persons of color* -Free persons of color are either emancipated slaves, or their descendants, or such persons as shall have at least one-eighth of Negro blood in their veins.

*Rights of free persons of color* -The free person of color is entitled to no right of citizenship, except such as are specially given by law. His status differs from that of the slave in this: No master having dominion over him. He *is entitled to the free use of his liberty, labor and property, except so far as he is restrained by law.*

*Included in slave laws* -All laws enacted in reference to slaves, and in their nature applicable to free persons of color, shall be construed to include them, unless specially excepted.

*Insurrection*- Insurrection shall consist in any combined resistance to the lawful authority of the master or the State, with intent to the permanent denial thereof, when the same is manifested or intended to be manifested by acts of violence— the mere resistance of a slave, or his attempt to escape, or actual escape, from the master, shall not constitute insurrection.

# Marriage and Family Codes

*1749*...No intermarriage between white people and negroes...

*1852*...Any white man, and woman of color, of any shade of complexion whatever, free or slave, who shall live together in a state of adultery or fornication, or of adultery and fornication as the case may be, and be indicted for the same, and on conviction shall be fined or imprisoned in the common jail of the county, or both, at the discretion of the Court...

*1853* ...That the children, not exceeding five years of age, of any woman slave, and such woman slave shall not be separately sold or exposed to sale by any executor, administrator, guardian or other trustee, nor shall they be separated in any division made by any executor, administrator, guardian or other trustee, but shall be placed together in one of the parts into which the estate to which they belong is to be divided, unless such division cannot in any wise be effected without such separation.

*1861*...*Any white woman within the limits of this State, who shall live or cohabit with any negro slave or free person of color, shall be guilty of adultery or fornication, on conviction, shall be fined or imprisoned in the common jail of the county, or both, at the discretion of the Court; and said slave or free person of color so found living or cohabiting with any white woman in this State, shall be imprisoned for one week, in the county jail, and receive, during said week, thirty-nine lashes on his bare back, on three separate days during said week...*

*1865*...*among persons of color, the parent shall be required to maintain his, or her children, whether legitimate or illegitimate...*

*1866*...*every colored child heretofore born, is declared to be the legitimate child of his mother, and also, of his colored father, if acknowledged by such father...*

...*An act to legalize marriages by colored ordained ministers of the gospel and also to authorize such colored ministers of African descent, to solemnize future marriages between freedmen and freedwomen of African descent only...*

...*Colored ministers of the gospel, of African descent, to celebrate marriages between freedmen and freedwomen, or persons of African descent only, under the same terms and regulations of this State for marriages between free white citizens...*

...*Persons of color, now living together as husband and wife, are hereby declared to sustain that legal relationship to each other....*

*1927...An Act to define who are persons of color and who are white persons, to prohibit and prevent the intermarriage of such persons...*

..."*All negroes, mulattoes, mustizos, and their descendants, having any ascertainable trace of either Negro or African, West Indian, or Asiatic Indian blood in their veins, and all descendants of any person having either Negro or African, West Indian, or Asiatic Indian blood in his or her veins, shall be known in this State as persons of color.*"

...*it shall be a felony for any person to willfully or knowingly make or cause to be made a registration certificate false as to color or race, and upon conviction thereof such person shall be punished by imprisonment...*

...*that from and after the passage of this Act it shall be unlawful for a white person to marry any save a white person. Any person, white or otherwise, who shall marry or go through a marriage ceremony in violation of this provision shall be guilty of a felony, and shall be punished by imprisonment...*

*...Be it further enacted that when any birth certificate is forwarded to the Bureau of Vital Statistics, showing the birth of a legitimate child to parents one of whom is white and one of whom is colored, it shall be the duty of the State Registrar of Vital Statistics to report the same to the Attorney-General of the State, with full information concerning the same. Thereupon it shall be the duty of the Attorney-General to institute criminal proceedings against the parents of such child, for any violation of the provisions of this Act which may have been committed...*

# Worship Codes

*1749...* In case of any contagious distempers on board, proper places must be appointed at a distance from the town for Sagrettos where the whole crew of ships and the Negroes may be lodged and supplied with refreshments and assisted towards their recovery... "No master shall oblige or even suffer his Negro or Negroes to work on the Lords Day, he shall permit or oblige them to attend at some time in that Day for instruction in the Christian Religion which the Protestant Ministers The Minister or Ministers shall on all occasion inculcate in the Negroes the natural obligations to a married state where there are female slaves cohabiting with them and an absolute forbearance of blaspheming the name of God by profane cursing or swearing...

*1833...*No person of color whether free or slave, shall be allowed to preach to exhort or join in any religious exercise, with any persons of color, either free or slave, there being more than seven persons of color present. They shall first obtain a written certificate from three ordained ministers of the gospel of their own order, license not to be for a longer term than six months, and to be revocable at any time by the persons granting it...

*1863*... The *General Assembly of Georgia section 1376 of the Code of Georgia, which reads as follows: "It shall be unlawful for any church, society, or other body, or any persons, to grant any license or other authority to any slave or free person of color to preach or exhort, or otherwise officiate in church matters," be, and the same is hereby repealed...*

# Business and Commerce Codes

*1799... Whereas many persons purchase provisions and other commodities from slaves, by which the owners of such slaves are, and may continue to be great sufferers, should such pernicious practices continue, any person or persons whatsoever, who shall purchase from, or sell to, for money, or barter with any slave or slaves for any sort of corn, rice, cotton or other commodities whatsoever, unless such slave or slaves shall produce a ticket, describing the article and quantity permitted to be sold, from his, her or their employer, owner or manager, allowing such slave or slaves to dispose of such money, or purchase or sell such provision or commodity, shall upon conviction before any court having competent jurisdiction thereof in the county where such offense shall be committed, forfeit the sum of three hundred dollars...*

*1803...Prohibits trading with slaves...*

*...If the owner or owners of any slave, shall permit such slave for a consideration or otherwise to have, hold and enjoy the privilege of laboring, or otherwise transacting business for his, her, or themselves, except on their own premises, such owner or owners shall, for every such weekly*

*offence, forfeit and pay the sum of $30.00 except in the cities of Savannah and Augusta, and the town of Sunbury...*

*1806...An act for the establishing and regulating patrols, and for preventing any person from purchasing provisions or any other commodities from, or selling such to any slave, unless such slave shall produce a ticket from his or her owner, manager or employer, fines imposed for the refusal and neglect of patrol any person liable to do and perform patrol duty, shall forfeit and pay a sum not exceeding five dollars for each offence...*

*1808...Any person or persons to keep a store, shop or tavern, and are retailers of spirituous liquors and other commodities, by which a former act obliges them to take out licenses -- shall be obliged on receiving such license, to take and subscribe the following oath or affirmation, before the clerk of the Inferior court: I A. B. do solemnly swear or affirm, as the case may be, that I will not either directly or indirectly, nor shall any person in my employ, with my desire, knowledge or approbation, deal, barter or trade with any negro slave for the article of provisions or otherwise, neither will I sell unto him, her or them, any spirituous liquors or mixture thereof, without the permission, or consent of the owners, agents, attorneys, or overseers of such slaves, as long as I continue in this State, and in the capacity of a retailer of*

12

merchandize, that if any retailer of spirituous liquors, or any other persons, shall sell to any slave any spirituous liquors or mixture thereof, or shall purchase from him, her or them any commodities without the license or consent of the owner, or such other persons who may have the care or government of such slaves, every person, so offending, shall forfeit the sum of thirty dollars...

*1816*...It shall not be lawful for any owner or Patroon of a Boat, to suffer or permit any boat hand or negro, being a slave, to put on board their boat, whereof he is owner or Patroon, any corn, cotton, peas or other article of produce, as the property of such boat hand or negro, for the purpose of carrying the same to Savannah or elsewhere to market, or for sale; nor shall such owner or patroon suffer the boat hands or other negroes, being slaves as aforesaid, on board of their boat or boats, to barter or trade, the one with the other, in any article of produce as before enumerated, under any pretext whatever...

...If any person or persons shall buy or receive from any slave or slaves, any Money, Cotton, Tobacco, Wheat, Rye, Oats or Corn, without a ticket authorizing such slave or slaves, to dispose of such money, specially specifying the sum so intended to be laid out, which such slave or slaves may intend to dispose of, from his, their owner or overseer or overseers, as the case may be, such person or persons so offending, shall forfeit and pay to the informer on conviction *thereof if any person, or persons, shall purchase any of the aforesaid articles, from any slave, or slaves, with or without a lawful ticket, after sunset, and before sun rise, or on the Sabbath day, he, she or they shall, if convicted, be fined by the Court the sum of Five Hundred Dollars, for each and every violation of this law...*

*1818 ...An act to prohibit slaves from selling certain commodities*

*If any slave or slaves, or free persons of color, shall purchase or buy any of the aforesaid commodities from any slave or slaves, he, she, or they, on conviction thereof, , shall receive on his, her, or their backs, thirty-nine lashes, to be well laid on by any constable of said county, or other person appointed by the justice of the peace nothing herein contained shall prevent any slave or slaves, from selling poultry at any time without a ticket, in the counties of Liberty, McIntosh, Camden, Glynn, and Wayne...*

*...No free person of color within the State, (Indians in amity with this State excepted,) shall be permitted to purchase or acquire any real estate, or any slave or slaves, either by a direct conveyance to such a free person of color of the legal title of such real estate, or slave or slaves, or by conveyance to any white person...*

*1824 ...That if any slave shall sell or purchase without a ticket authorizing him so to do, any quantity or amount whatever of cotton,* tobacco, wheat, rye, oats, corn, rice or poultry, or any other articles except such as are known to be usually manufactured or vended by slaves, they shall suffer the pains provided by an act passed the nineteenth day of December eighteen hundred and eighteen, entitled an act to alter and amend an act to prohibit slaves from selling certain commodities therein mentioned...

*1826*...That from and after the passage of this act, shall not be lawful for any merchant, shopkeeper, or any persons whatever, to trade with any slave or slaves, free negroes or mulattoes, with or without a ticket, after sunset or before sunrise in the county of Liberty. If any slave or slaves, free negroes or mulattoes, shall be seen in any store, shop, or tippling house, with any articles of sale within the aforesaid prohibited hours, it shall be taken and received as evidence against the person or persons owning, or person keeping the store, shop, or tippling house, of a violation of this act: Provided nevertheless, that nothing herein contained shall be so as to prevent the owner or owners of said store, shop, or tippling house, from supplying any written order of the owner, overseer, or manager of any such slave or slaves, free negroes or mulattoes...

... if any slave or slaves, free negroes or mulattoes, shall be seen in any store, shop, or tipling house, with any articles of sale within the aforesaid prohibited hours, it shall be taken and received as evidence against the person or persons owning, or person keeping the store, shop, or tippling house, of a violation of this act...

*1834*...no free person of colour shall have and maintain or occupy any house in the town of Greenesborough, or in the town of Madison, for the purpose of keeping and maintaining a public eating-establishment...

*1835*...Every druggist or apothecary, vending any medicines of a poisonous quality, shall not vend the same to any person or persons of color...

*1839*...it shall be lawful for any free person or persons of color, in the city of Darien, to hold real estate in the name of his, her or their guardian, in trust, however, and for the only use, benefit and be hoof of any such free person or persons of color...

...it shall not be lawful for any free person of color or slave to keep a house of entertainment...

...no slave shall be allowed to hire his or her time from his or her owner or manager; nor shall any slave be allowed to work or carry on any traffic upon his or her own account, or for the purpose of procuring a livelihood...

*1841*...An act to prohibit from sale, or gift, all printed or written books, papers, pamphlets, writing paper, ink, and all other articles of stationery of any kind whatever to any slave or free persons of color in this State...

*1843*...all white persons residing in said town (Cassville)..., shall pay a poll-tax to said town, of fifty cents, ... and all free persons of color residing, or who may hereafter reside in said town, over the age of twenty-one years, shall in like manner pay a town tax of two dollars...

*1845*...Act to prohibit colored mechanics and masons, being slaves or free persons of color being mechanics or masons, from making contracts for the erection of buildings, or for the repairs of buildings, and declaring the white person directly or indirectly contracting with or employing them...

*1850*...each and every male citizen between the ages of twenty-one and sixty, be taxed annually the sum of twenty-five cents only.... And be it further enacted, That each and every free negro or free person of color in this State, between the ages of eighteen and fifty, shall be taxed annually the sum of five dollars...

...each negro or person of color nominally a slave... shall pay the tax of one hundred and fifty dollars as above...

...Prohibiting the introduction of slaves into this State for the purpose of sale, and all prohibiting the sale, offer to sell, or the purchase of slaves at any time after their introduction into this State, have been repealed by the present General Assembly; and whereas the only legitimate object of punishment, the prevention of crime, ceases with the abolition of the crime itself...

*1863*...That from and after the passage of this Act, if any person shall violate the provisions of the one thousand eight hundred and fifty-fifth (1855) paragraph of the revised Code of Georgia, he, she, or they shall be punished by fine, at the discretion of the Court. Sec. 1855 of Code provides, that each owner shall keep his slaves on his own, or within his control. Shall not permit them to labor or transact business on holidays, or on his own premises. Nor to rent any house, room, store or land their own account...

*1866*... That persons of color shall have the right to make and enforce contracts, to sue and be sued; to be parties and give evidence to inherit, purchase, lease, sell, hold and convey, real and personal property, and to have full and equal benefit of all laws and proceedings...

*1925...No license to operate a Billiard Room shall be issued to any person ...of the White or Caucasian race to operate a Billiard Room to be used by, frequented or patronized by persons of the Negro race; or to any person of the Negro race to operate a Billiard Room to be used by, frequented or patronized by persons of the White or Caucasian race...*

Power concedes nothing without a demand.
It never did and it never will.

Frederick Douglas

# Sale and Purchase of Blacks

*1805*...No administrator shall be allowed to sell any slave or slaves belonging to the estate of his intestate, but where the other personal estate, together with the hire of such slave or slaves for twelve months, shall be insufficient to discharge the debts due by the estate, or where one or more slaves shall be subject to distribution and an equal division thereof cannot be made in kind, it shall be lawful for the court of ordinary, by which administration was granted, to direct the sale of such slave or slaves...

*1808*... Be it enacted that John Landrum, of the county of Wilkes be, and he is hereby permitted to bring into this state three negro slaves, already purchased by him in the state of Virginia, and to possess, hold and enjoy said negroes, free from all suits, prosecutions or fines imposed by an act entitled an act to prohibit the further importation of slaves into this state...

*1812*...An Act To compel citizens of the different counties in this state, as well as citizens of other states who do now or hereafter may own slaves residing in the county of Scriven, to make a return of, and pay taxes on all such slaves...

*1831*...An act to authorize the Justices of the Inferior Court of Wilkes county, or a majority of them, to hire or purchase negroes, for the improvement of the Roads and Bridges in said county...

*1832*...from and immediately after the passage of this act, it shall be the duty of the Sheriff of the county of Jefferson to advertise for sale on the first Tuesday of the month a certain slave that has been confined in the Jail of that county for twelve months, first giving thirty days notice of such sale in one of the public; papers of this State which advertisement shall contain a description of the name, age and height of said slave...

...when a runaway slave is committed to any jail in this State, it shall be the duty of the Jailor to prepare a notice containing a fair description of the name, age and height, and complexion of said slave, together with the time of his commitment, & the name of the person to whom said slave reports himself to belong; if no person appears and claims said slave after he or she has been advertised as aforesaid -- then it shall be the duty of said jailor to give notice thereof to the justices of the inferior court of said county, who shall cause said slave to be levied on by the Sheriff of said county as a runaway slave, and advertised to be sold on the first Tuesday in the month...

*1849*...*An act to alter and amend an act to incorporate the Southern Mutual Insurance Company, ...Said corporation may insure, for any term not exceeding ten years... the lives of slaves against death, such damage, loss or death, not resulting from the carelessness, negligence or design of the party insured, and to any amount not exceeding three-fourths of the value of the property insured...*

*1865*...*Whereas, during the late war the State of Georgia has been overrun by the opposing armies; ...the accumulated capital of nearly a century, represented by slave labor, amounting to nearly three hundred millions of dollars, has been destroyed, and the prospect of successful agriculture, the basis of all value, now dependent on the voluntary labor of the freedmen, is a question of doubt and experiment, therefore:... there shall be no levy or sale of property, of defendants in this State, under any execution, founded on any judgment, order or decree of any Court heretofore, or hereafter to be rendered, upon any contract or liability, made or incurred prior to the 1st June 1865...*

*1917*... *Whereas the only relief that can be suggested for the United States Government through the Congress, the law making provision to provide for the payment of a sufficient sum through the Treasury Department of each State* to amply provide for the old slaves who are now unable to work for a support which his master was compelled to give him by the State, and to furnish a sufficient sum to each State to be used to pay pensions fixed by the laws of each State to each Confederate soldier and to the widows of such soldiers as are now provided for by the States...

...Resolved, second, that a fair and just pension should be made by the United States Government to each negro man and woman born and reared in slavery and now too old to work, who by emancipation lost the protecting care and comfort which in times of slavery the laws of every Southern State required the master to bestow upon him or her...

## Revised Code

...Slaves may be brought into this state from any other slave holding state of this confederacy; but no Negroes, or other slaves, shall be imported into this state either as slaves or apprentices, from their native land, or any foreign country; and all such Negroes, so illegally imported into this state and place under the control of the executive of this state, shall be sold by his order under such regulations as he may prescribe...

# *Employment Codes*

*1806*...*it shall not be lawful for any negro slave or other person of color, to have the command, or to act as patroon of any boat carrying goods, wares and merchandize, or produce, from either of the said cities (Savannah and Augusta) to the other...*

*1807*...*Citizens of Savannah, Augusta heretofore, and do now experience great injury and inconvenience from the number of free negroes, mulattoes or mustizoes of vicious and loose habits who have settled and daily settling therein, who may then or at any time thereafter, reside with in the corporate limits of the cities Savannah and Augusta, any person who hires or let any house or tenement to any free negro, mulatto or mustizoes within the limits of said cities, without permissionfrom the city council thereof, shall be subject to the same penalties as if such house or tenement had been let or hired to a slave...*

*1818*...*All and every person of color (Indians in amity with this State, or regularly articled seamen or apprentices arriving in any ship or vessel excepted) who shall, after the first Monday in May next, be found within the limits of this*

State, whose names shall not be enrolled in the book of registry, described in the proceeding section, or having been enrolled, who shall have been refused certificates in the manner therein prescribed, and who shall be working at large, enjoying the profits of his or her labor, and not in the employment of a master or owner, or of some white person, by and in virtue of an actual and bona fide contract, with the master or owner of such person of color, securing to such master or owner the profits arising from the labor of such person of color, shall be deemed, held, and taken to be slaves...

*1821*... That from and after the passing of this act it shall be lawful for the Commissioners of Pilotage to employ Henry Drummond, a free man of colour, for the pilotage of vessels to and from the Port of Darien...

*1829*...All ships or vessels coming into any part of this State by sea from any port or place in any other State, or any foreign country, having on board any free negro or free person of color employed as a steward, mariner, or any other capacity, or as a passenger, shall be subject to quarantine for the space of forty days...

...Be it enacted, that no slave or free person of color shall be employed in the setting of types, in any printing office of this State...

*1830*...It shall not be lawful for any owner or manager of any slave or slaves in the county of Twiggs, to allow him or them to hire his or their own time, to live on a separate town lot, from his owner or manager, or to hire themselves on any farm or plantation, or hire any slave or slaves to any other person to the intent that said slaves, may be allowed to live separate and apart from their owner or manager, or to be allowed to furnish victuals for sale or accommodation of any person or persons whatsoever, and that any owner or manager offending against this act, shall be deemed and considered guilty of a misdemeanor...

*1832*...That no slave shall be allowed to hire his, or her time, from his or her owner or manager, nor shall any slave be allowed to work or carry on any traffic upon his or her own account, or for the purpose of procuring a livelihood or raising money to pay his or her hire or wages to his or her owner or employer in said counties; except such as may be barbers, who shall be permitted to hire their time, and rent shops for carrying on their business...

*1834*...from and immediately after the passage of this act, Henry Adams, a free person of colour, who is now residing without the limits *of the State of Georgia, but who is a native of the same, and a regularly ordained preacher of the Gospel, of the Baptist order, be, and he is hereby permitted to labor in the ministry within the limits of the State of Georgia...*

*1835...Nothing in this Act shall be so construed as to prevent druggists and apothecaries from employing any negro or free person of color in that branch of their business which does not require them to open their drugs or medicines, or compound or dispense the same, but they may be permitted to employ said persons to perform the laborious part of their work under the immediate direction and control of some white person...*

*1857 ... Free negro who, after being notified or warned to meet and work on such part or section of any of the public roads, to which he or they shall be assigned or appointed under this Act, shall neglect or refuse to obey such summons or warning, he or they shall, for each day he or they shall refuse or neglect to meet and work as aforesaid, be fined in a sum not exceeding two dollars...*

*...Every free negro and male slave above sixteen years, and under fifty years of age, within the county aforesaid, shall be and are hereby declared obliged to appear with such implements as are required, and work on the several roads,*

causeways and bridges, to which they may be severally allotted or appointed by the commissioners under this act...

...it shall be lawful for the Commissioners of Pilotage for the port of Darien, in the county of McIntosh, and State of Georgia, appointed to regulate the pilotage of vessels to and from said port, to invest Francis Cardone, a free man of color, with such authority to act as pilot, in said port of Darien...

## Revised codes

...Any white person who shall contract or bargain with any slave mechanic or mason, for erection or repairs of any building, whether the same be done directly or indirectly, shall be guilty of a misdemeanor...

"Before the Pilgrims landed at Plymouth, we were here. Before the pen of Jefferson etched across the pages of history the majestic words of the Declaration of Independence, we were here. If the inexpressible cruelties of slavery could not stop us, the opposition we now face will surely fail."

Martin Luther King, Jr.

"An individual who breaks a law that conscience tells him is unjust, and who willingly accepts the penalty of imprisonment in order to arouse the conscience of the community over its injustice, is in reality expressing the highest respect for the law."

Martin Luther King, Jr.

# Segregation Codes

*1830*...An act to provide for taking the Census of the State of Georgia distinguishing therein in separate columns, the free white persons from those of color, the slaves from citizens...

*1870*... the different railroads in this State acting as public carriers be required to furnish equal accommodations to all. without regard to race, color or previous condition, when a greater sum of fare is exacted than was demanded prior to January 1, 1861, which was at that date half fare for persons of color...

*1890*...An Act to amend the registration law of Pierce county, Georgia ...said registrar shall enter the names of such persons as registered in his book of registration in alphabetical order, keeping separate lists of white voters and separate lists of the colored voters...

*1891*...It unlawful for white and colored convicts to be confined together or work chained together...

*1894*...*Race to be noted on Book.* For the purpose of more easily identifying voters, the officers in charge of the voters book shall note thereon, in connection with each signature, the race of the person signing—that is to say, whether white or colored...

*1899*... from and after the passage of this Act sleeping-car companies and railroad companies operating sleeping-cars in this State ... shall separate the white and colored races in making said assignments, and the conductor and other employees on the train of cars to which said sleeping-car or cars may be attached, shall not permit white and colored passengers to occupy the same compartment...

... nothing in this Act shall be construed to compel sleeping-car companies or railroads operating sleeping-cars to carry persons of color in sleeping or parlor-cars; provided, that this Act shall not apply to colored nurses or servants traveling with their employers...

...any conductor or other employee of any sleeping-car, as well as any conductor or other employee of the train to which any sleeping-car may be attached, are hereby empowered with full police power to enforce the preceding section...

*1914*...the mayor and council shall have power to segregate the different races of people within said city limits, both as regards their places of residence and the business, trades or professions in which they may engage; they shall have power to prescribe the territory to be occupied by the different races as to their places of abode and their various callings and to prevent members of other races from living or carrying on any kind of business in such prescribed territory....

*1929*...Motor carriers may confine themselves to carrying either white or colored passengers, or they may provide different motor-vehicles for carrying white and colored passengers; and they may carry white and colored passengers in the same vehicle, but only under such conditions of separation of the races as the commission may prescribe...

*1979*...Codes relating to "the registration of individuals as to race; the prohibition of miscegenation; who may perform colored marriages; the criminal penalties invoked for allowing miscegenation to occur; the criminal penalty for false statement in application for marriage license" were repealed...

"If we accept and acquiesce in the face of discrimination, we accept the responsibility ourselves. We should, therefore, protest openly everything ... that smacks of discrimination or slander."

"For I am my mother's daughter, and the drums of Africa still beat in my heart. They will not let me rest while there is a single Negro boy or girl without a chance to prove his worth."

Mary McCleod Bethune

# Education Codes

*1833... If any person shall teach any slave, negro, or free person of colour, to read or write, either written or printed characters, or shall procure, suffer, or permit, a slave, negro, or person of colour, to transact business for him in writing, such person so offending, shall be guilty of a misdemeanor...*

*1866... WHO MAY BE THE SCHOLARS ...any free white inhabitant, being a citizen of the United States and of this State, and residing within the limits of any county or school district organized under this act, between the ages of six and twenty-one years, and any disabled and indigent soldier of this State, under thirty years of age, shall be entitled to instruction in the Georgia school of said county or district without charge for tuition or incidental expenses...*

*1870... it shall be the duty of the trustees, in their respective districts, to make all necessary arrangements for the instruction of the white and colored youth of the district in separate schools. ...the children of the white and colored races shall not be taught together in any sub-district of the State...*

*1890...Be it further enacted, That there shall be two boards of school trustees.... Said Board of Trustees shall consist one of three whites who shall act for the white school, and one of three negroes who shall act for the negro school, and that said white board shall be chosen by the white voters of said town, and that the negro board shall be chosen by negro voters of said town...*

*....said Board of Education shall be authorized to devise, design and adopt a plan of public instruction in said town, and modify the same from time to time; establish schools as they may deem proper, not exceeding one for the white race and one for the colored race, but no white child shall be taught in the colored school, and no colored child in the white school...*

*1898...the pro rata amount raised from such levy upon the property of the negro shall be used to establish and maintain public schools for the negro; and the money thus raised by levy upon the property of the whites shall be used to establish and maintain public schools for white persons...*

*1917...An act to establish and organize an agricultural, industrial, and normal school in this State as a branch of the University of Georgia...it* is hereby enacted by the authority of the same, That the Governor is hereby authorized to establish and cause to be maintained in some county as hereinafter provided, an agricultural, industrial and normal school for the training of the colored teachers of this State...

*1949*... Teacher-pupil ratios shall be determined separately for Whites and Negroes...

*1955*...no State or local funds derived from taxation or otherwise, shall be appropriated, paid out, used, or in any wise expended, directly or indirectly for the maintenance, upkeep, operation, or support of any public school district or system in this State which does not provide separate schools for white and colored children throughout the entire district or system and in which all the white and colored children attending public schools do not attend separate schools;

...nor shall any such money be appropriated, used, paid out, or in any wise expended, directly or indirectly, for the payment of any salary or compensation of any nature or character whatsoever to any teacher, instructor, employee or official of any public school district or system instructing mixed classes of white and colored children...

"I freed a thousand slaves I could have freed a thousand more if only they knew they were slaves."


"Never wound a snake; kill it."

Harriet Tubman

# Military Codes

*1813...That it shall not be lawful for any captain or commanding officer of a company in this state to enroll any free negro or mulatto, or suffer them to stand in ranks, whereby they may be instructed in military tactics or arts of warfare...*

*1878...Any person capable of doing military duty (not under 16 years of age) may be enrolled as a volunteer; but every company and battalion must be composed of men of the same race and color...*

*1884...The Georgia Volunteers shall consist of not exceeding fifty companies of infantry, seven companies of cavalry, and three companies of artillery, and the Georgia Volunteers, colored, of not more than twenty companies of infantry, one of cavalry, one of artillery...*

*...Battalions of colored troops, or persons of African descent, must be numbered in a separate series, describing them as such, and all volunteer troops of this State, of all arms and colors...*

*1893...in time of peace the aforesaid volunteer forces shall consist of not exceeding seventy-two companies of infantry, white, and twenty companies of infantry, colored; twenty-four troops of cavalry, white, and one troop of cavalry, colored; two batteries of artillery, white, and one battery of artillery, colored; not exceeding six machine gun platoons, white; a medical department, white; a hospital and ambulance corps, white; and to each regiment of infantry and cavalry, white,*

*...battalions of infantry, colored, may consist of not less than three nor more than six companies each...*


*1899...the military forces of this State shall be the active militia of this State, of which the white forces shall be known and designated as the "Georgia State Troops," and the colored forces as the "Georgia State Troops, Colored."*

*... in time of peace the aforesaid military forces shall consist of not exceeding sixty companies of infantry, white, and seven companies of infantry, colored; twelve troops of cavalry, white; two batteries of artillery, white, one battery of artillery, colored...*

*...Be it further enacted by authority aforesaid, That upon any occasion, whatsoever, when the Georgia State troops, and the Georgia State troops, colored, shall join together for duty, the senior officer of the Georgia State troops then present shall command the whole...*

# Conduct and
# Punishment Codes

*1765...It is absolutely necessary for the
security of his majesty's subject of this
providence and for preventing the many dangers
and inconveniences that may rise form the
disorderly and unlawful meetings of negroes and
other slaves within the same, that patrols should
be established, under proper regulations...*

*... Every patrol shall go to, and examine the
several plantations in their divisions and may and
shall take up all slaves which they shall see
without the fences or cleared ground of their
owners' plantation, who have not a ticket or
letter, or other token, to show the reasonableness
of their absence, or who have not some white
person in company to give and account of his,
her, or their business: and such patrol may
correct every such slave or slaves by whipping
with a switch, whip, or cow skin, not exceeding
twenty lashes.*

*1768...Immediately from and after passing
of this act, it shall not be lawful for any slave,
unless in the presence of some white person, to
carry and make use of fire arms, or any offensive
weapon whatsoever, unless such slave shall have
a ticket or license in writing, from his master,*

*mistress, or overseer, to hunt and kill game, cattle...*

*1770...Every owner or owners who may keep on any plantation the number of ten slaves or more, over the age of sixteen, shall be compelled to keep a white man capable of bearing arms, as an overseer...*

*...All negroes, Indians, mulattoes, or mestizoes, who now are, or hereafter shall be in this province and all their offspring born, or to be born, shall be, and they are hereby declared to be, and remain forever hereafter absolute slaves, and shall follow the condition of the mother, and shall be taken and deemed in law to be chattels personal in the hands of their respective owners or possessors, and their executors, administrators, and assigns, to all intents and purposes whatsoever...*

*1793...An act to prevent the importation of negroes into this state from the places herein mentioned, that all free negroes, mulattoes, mustizoes, who at any time after the passing of this act shall continue into this state, shall, within thirty days of their arrival, enroll him, her or themselves in the clerks office of the county wherein they reside; and within six months thereafter procure a certificate of two or more magistrates of the county, failure of such enrollment ... he, she or they, shall be subject to be taken up and committed to the nearest jail, for a term not exceeding three months...*

*1799...if any person or persons whomsoever, shall maliciously deprive a slave or slaves of life, he, she or they so offending, shall be prosecuted except in case of insurrection by such slave, and unless such death should happen by accident, in giving such slave moderate correction...*

*1801...it shall not be lawful for any person to manumit or set free any negro slave or slaves, mulatto, mustizo, or any other person or persons of color, who may be deemed slaves at the time of this Act, in any other manner or form, than by an application to the Legislature for that purpose. That if any person or persons shall after the passing of this Act, set any slave or slaves, in any other manner or form than the one prescribed herein, he shall forfeit for every offence two hundred dollars...*

*1805...if any slave who shall be in the lawful business or service of his or her master, owner, overseer or other person having the charge, care and management of such slave, shall be beaten, bruised, wounded, maimed or disabled, by any person or persons not having sufficient cause for so doing, every person or persons so offending shall be liable to indictment in the superior court...*

*1806...If any slave, free negro, Indian, mulatto or mustizo, (Indians in amity with the United States excepted) shall be guilty of homicide of any sort, upon any white person, except by misadventure, or, if a slave, in defense of his or her owner, or other person under whose care and government such slave shall be, or shall raise or attempt to raise any insurrection, or commit or attempt to commit any rape on any white person whomsoever, every such offender or offenders, his and their abiders and abettors, shall upon conviction thereof, suffer death; or if any slave, free negro, Indian, mulatto or mustizo, (except shall willfully and maliciously kill any slave, free negro, Indian, mulatto or mustizo, or shall break open, burn or destroy any dwelling-house or other building whatsoever, or set fire to any rice, corn or other grain, tar kiln, barrel or barrels of pitch, tar, turpentine, rosin, or any other goods or commodities whatsoever, or shall steal any goods or chattels whatsoever, or inveigle, delude or entice any slave or slaves to run away, whereby the owner or owners of such slave or slaves, shall, might, or would have lost or been deprived of such slave or slaves, every such slave, free negro, Indian, mulatto or mustizo, and his and their accomplices, abiders and abettors, shall upon conviction as aforesaid, suffer death, or such other punishment as the justices and jury shall in their discretion think fit...*

...any person liable to do and perform patrol duty, as prescribed in the above recited act, who shall refuse or neglect to do and perform the same, shall forfeit and pay a sum not exceeding five dollars for each offence...

*1807*... That the power and authority vested in the said commissioners, shall not extend to the passing of any byelaws or ordinances, which may require corporal punishment to be inflicted (except the said corporal punishment is to be inflicted upon slaves or other persons of color)...

... The fine for negroes, not working on the roads in the aforesaid of Chatham, and Essingham, shall after the passing of this act, the sum of two dollars, for each and every day that any negro subject to work on roads, shall fail so to do...

... Whereas the citizens of Savannah, Augusta...have heretofore, and do now experience great injury and inconvenience from the number of free negroes, mulattoes and mustizoes of vicious and loose habits who have settled and are daily settling therein... Be it therefore enacted that from and after the first day of January next...any person who shall hire or let any house or tenement to any free negroe, mulatto or mustizoes within the limits of said cities, ...shall be subject to the same penalties as if such house or tenement had been let or hired to a slave...

*1810...A white person resident, may be appointed his or her guardian; of such free person of color...*

*...All free persons of color (native Indians excepted) who shall arrive in this state, shall within ten days after his or her arrival, except in a county in which there is a sea-port town, where two days shall be allowed and no more, register his or her name with the Clerk of the Superior court of the county in which he or she shall have arrived, declare to the said Clerk his or her occupation or calling, the place of his or her residence and birth, the place from whence he or she shall last have come, the object for which he or she shall have come into this state, and the name of the person or persons in whose employment or service he or she may be engaged. If any free person of color coming into this state after the first day of March aforesaid, shall neglect or refuse to comply with the aforesaid provisions of this act (native Indians excepted) forfeit & pay for every such neglect or refusal, the sum of thirty dollars...*

*1811...In case it should appear to them after investigation, that the crime or crimes wherewith such slave or slaves stand charged, is a crime or crimes for which he, she or they ought to suffer death, such slave or slaves, that the said jurors by their verdict shall say whether such slave or slaves are guilty or not guilty, and if a verdict of guilty should be returned by such jury, the court* shall immediately pronounce sentence of death by hanging or such other punishment not amounting to death...

$1815$...Prohibits the Clerks of the several Courts of Ordinary from recording any deed of manumission or other paper which shall have for object, the manumitting and setting free any slave or slaves, under a certain penalty for so doing, so far as the same relates or is construed to relate to last Wills and Testaments, be and the same is hereby repealed...

...It shall be the duty of the Inferior courts of the several counties in this state, on receiving information on oath of any infirm slave or slaves being in a suffering situation from the neglect of the owner or owners of such slave or slaves, to make particular enquiries into the situation of such slave or slaves, and render such relief as they in their discretion may think proper, the said Courts may, and they are hereby authorized, to sue for and recover from the owner or owners of such slave or slaves, the amount that may be appropriated for the relief of such slave or slaves...

$1816$... The following shall be considered as capital offences, when committed by a slave or *free person of color; - insurrection, or any attempt to excite it; poisoning, or attempting to poison; committing a rape, or attempting it, on a free white female; assaulting a free white person, with intent to murder or with a weapon likely to produce death; maiming a free white person; - burglary, or arson of any description, as contained in the penal code of this State; murder of another slave, or free person of color; - every, and each of these offences shall, upon conviction, be punished with death...*

*...And if any free person of color commits the offence of inveigling, or enticing away any slave or slaves, for the purpose of, and with the intention to aid and assist such slave or slaves, leaving the service of his or her owner or owners, or in going to another State; such person so offending shall, for each and every such offence, on conviction, be confined in the penitentiary at hard labor for one year, and at the expiration of their imprisonment, shall be sold to the highest bidder as a slave, for and during the term of their natural lives...*

*...Commissioners shall have full power and authority, to appoint, from among the persons residing within the limits of said corporation, a patrol, or patrols for said corporation, at such times, and on such occasions, as they may deem proper -- provided, that one person, at least, of those composing such patrol or patrols, shall be a slave holder, and that no punishment inflicted by such patrol or patrols, on any slave or slaves, shall*

exceed moderate correction -- Provided also, that all and every person or persons who shall refuse to do patrol duty when required as aforesaid, shall, without good excuse, to be rendered to said commissioners, be liable to be fined by said commissioners, in any sum not exceeding five dollars...

...Killing a slave in the act of revolt, or when the said slave resists a legal arrest, shall be justifiable homicide...

...If any person or persons shall by any enticement, or by giving a pass, or by any other means, induce a slave or slaves to runaway from his, her, or their owner or owners, with an intention feloniously to sell said slave or slaves, or otherwise to deprive the said owner or owners of the services of said slave or slaves, such person or persons, so offending, shall pay the value of said slave or slaves, to the owner or owners thereof; and also be punished by imprisonment at hard labor for any time not less than three years nor longer than seven years...

...Persons having one-eighth, or more, of negro or African blood in their veins, are not white persons in the meaning of this Code...

...Any person may take up any negroes that shall be found out of the plantation or place where they belong, or incorporated town where they reside, acting unlawfully, or under suspicious circumstances, and if found with an offensive weapon shall take the same away, and if the negro is insolent, or refuses to answer, may whip said negro as the patrol may...

... A slave committing a crime not punishable with death or perpetual imprisonment, by the threats, command or coercion of his or her owner, or any person exercising or assuming authority over such slave, shall not be found guilty...

...Any person, (except the owner,) beating, whipping, or wounding a slave, or beating, whipping or wounding a free person of colour, without sufficient cause, or provocation being first given by such slave or free person of colour, may be indicated, and on conviction, shall be fined at the discretion of the court...

...Any owner or owners of a slave or slaves, who shall cruelly treat such slave or slaves, by unnecessary and excessive whippings, by withholding proper food and sustenance, by requiring greater labor from such slave or slaves, than he, she or they are able to perform, by not affording proper clothing, whereby the health of such slave or slaves may be injured and impaired -- every such owner or owners shall upon sufficient information being laid before the grand jury...,who on conviction, shall be sentenced to pay a fine...

...if any slave, or slaves, mulatto or free person of color, shall purchase any of said commodities, from any slave, or slaves,... he, she or they, shall on conviction thereof, ...receive on his, her or their bare-back, thirty-nine lashes, to be well laid on by any constable of said court...

...If any person shall take money, goods, chattels, lands or other reward, on promise thereof to compound any treason, exciting or attempting to stir up and excite an insurrection or revolt of slaves, murder, manslaughter, rape, sodomy, arson, forgery, burglary, house-breaking, robbery, larceny, receiving stolen goods or other property, escape, rescue, breach of prison, bribery, perjury or subordination of perjury, or any other offence heretofore denominated felony, or any offence punishable in this code with imprisonment in the penitentiary...

...No congregation or company of slaves, exceeding seven males in number, shall, under any pretence, except for Divine worship, assemble themselves outside of any incorporated town, and then they must be under the control and presence of as many as five citizens of the neighborhood, except slaves who may assemble on their masters' premises when he or his overseer is present...

*1817*... That in all cases where the jury, on the trial of any slave or free person of color, shall return a verdict of guilty, the court shall pass the sentence of death on such slave or free person of color...

*...If any person shall conceal, harbor, hide, or cause to be concealed, harbored or hidden, any slave or slaves, to the injury of the owner or owners thereof, such persons so offending, shall on conviction, be sentenced to be imprisoned in the Penitentiary at hard labor, for any period of time not exceeding two years...*

*...It shall not be lawful, for any person or persons whatsoever, to bring, import or introduce into this state, to aid or assist, or knowingly to become concerned or interested, in bringing, importing, or introducing into this state, either by land or by water, or in any manner whatsoever, any slave or slaves...*
*...Provided always, that this act shall not extend to any citizen of this state,... nor to any citizen of any other state, ... who shall bring, import, or introduce into this state, any slave or slaves for the sole purpose of being held to service or labor... and without the intent to sell, transfer, barter, lend, hire, mortgage, procure to be taken or sold under execution or other legal process,...*
*And provided further, that this act shall not extend to prevent any person traveling into this state from bringing therein any such slave or slaves as may be needful for his comfortable and usual attendance upon his journey, nor to any person or persons bringing into this state any slave or slaves, found on board any ship or vessel which may be taken as a prize of war...*

...An Act For disposing of any such negro, mulatto or person of color, who has been or may hereafter be imported or brought into this state, in violation of an act of the United States, entitled, an act to prohibit the importation of slaves into any port or place within the jurisdiction of the United States, from and after the first day of January, 1808. And be it further enacted, That His Excellency the Governor is hereby empowered to cause the said negroes, mulattoes or persons of color to be sold, after giving sixty days notice in a public gazette...


... Exciting an insurrection or revolt of slaves, or any attempt by writing, speaking or otherwise, to excite an insurrection or revolt of slaves, shall be punished with death...


*1818*...All and every free person or persons of color, residing or being within this State, at the time of the passing of this act, shall, on or before that day, and annually on or before the first Monday in March in each and every succeeding year, which they shall continue within the limits of this State, make application to the clerk of the inferior court of the county in which they reside, and it shall be the duty of said clerk to make a registry of such free person or persons of color, in a book by him to be kept for that purpose, particularly describing therein the names, ages, places of nativity and residence, time of coming *into this State, and occupation or pursuit of such free person or persons of color...*

*1821...The following be considered as capital offences, when committed by a slave or free person of color: insurrection, or an attempt to excite it; committing a rape or attempting it on a free white person or female; murder or a free white person; or murder of a slave or free person of color, or poisoning of a human being; every and each of these offences shall, on conviction, be punished with death; also be considered as capital offences, when committed by a slave or free person of color: assaulting a free white person with intent to murder, or with a weapon likely to produce death; maiming a free white person; burglary or arson of any description; also any attempt to poison a human being;, on conviction, be punished with death, the punishment shall be by whipping, at the discretion of court, and branding on the cheek with a letter M...*

*...That the said board may, within the corporate limits of the said town, make all needful regulations for the restraint and punishment of slaves and free persons of color and for the exclusive government of patrols therein...*

*...If any person or persons shall be convicted of fishing or attempting to fish with any of the instruments, or within the time herein before*

forbidden, and being thereof duly convicted, shall forfeit and pay for every such offence the sum of thirty dollars when the offender or offenders should be slaves, then, in that case, He, she or they, so offending, shall receive on his, her or their bare backs twenty lashes; if the person or persons so offending should be a free person of color, then, and in that case, he, she or they shall receive on his, her or their bare backs thirty-nine lashes...

*1823*...Every owner or owners, who may keep on any plantation the number of ten slaves or more, over the age of sixteen, shall be compelled to keep a white man capable of bearing arms, as an manager, or superintendent on said plantation...

*1826*... if any captain of a vessel, or other person or persons shall transport, entice, carry away or inveigle, or shall attempt to transport, entice, carry away, or inveigle, or shall aid, abet, or in anywise assist or be [Illegible Text] in the transportation, removal, enticing, inveigling, or going, running, or carrying away out of the State of Georgia of any free person of color or any other person of color, claiming or pretending to claim to be free, who shall not have such genuine certificate of registry of freedom duly issued to him or her as aforesaid, such person or persons so offending shall be liable to be indicted as for a misdemeanor, and shall be punished by imprisonment in the common jail...

...no colored seaman arriving from any port whatever (except from ports in South Carolina) shall be permitted to leave the vessel in which they have arrived, in any port in this state, from the hours of six o'clock in the evening until five o'clock in the succeeding morning...

*1829*...If any slave, negro, or free person of color, or any white person, shall teach any other slave, negro, or free person of color, to read or write either written or printed characters, the said free person of color or slave shall be punished by fine and whipping, or fine or whipping at the discretion of the court; and if a white person so offending, he, she, or they shall be punished with fine...

...From and after the passing of this act, the willful and malicious burning or setting fire to, or attempting to burn a house in a city, town, or village, when committed by a slave or free person of color, shall be punished with death; the willful and malicious burning a dwelling-house on a farm or plantation, or elsewhere (not in a city, town, or village), or the setting fire thereto in the night-time, when said house is actually occupied

56

by a person or persons, with the intent to burn the same, when committed by a slave or free person of color, shall be punished with death...

...if any free negro or person of colour, so coming in the said ship or vessel, shall come on shore or have any communication with any person of colour [Illegible Text] in this State, while the said ship or vessel shall be riding quarantine as aforesaid, such negro or person of colour, shall be immediately apprehended and committed to the common jail...

... every free negro or person of colour coming into this State as aforesaid, and who shall not depart the State, in case of the captain refusing or neglecting to carry him away, within ten days after the vessel in which he came has departed, shall be liable on conviction before any Magistrate of the county, to be whipped not exceeding thirty-nine lashes...

...if any slave, negro, mustizo, or free person of colour, or any other person, shall circulate, bring or cause to be circulated or brought into this state or aid or assist in any manner, or be instrumental in aiding or assisting in the circulation or bringing into this state, or in any manner concerned in any printed or written pamphlet, paper or circular, for the purposes of exciting to insurrection, conspiracy or resistance among the slaves, negroes, or free persons of colour, of this state, against their owners or the citizens of this state, the said person or persons *offending against this section of this act, shall be punished with death...*

*1832...* When a runaway slave is committed to any jail in this State, it shall be the duty of the jailor to prepare a notice containing a fair description of the name, age and height, and complexion of said slave, together with the time his commitment, and the name of the person to whom said slave reports himself to belong, which notice shall be published in one of the Milledgeville papers, and such other paper as said jailor may direct, if no person appears to claim and prove property in said slave, then it shall be the duty of said sheriff to sell said slave for cash to the highest bidder...

*1833...* from and after the passage of this act, it shall not be lawful for any free person of colour in this state, to own, use, or carry fire arms of any description whatever...

*1834...* no free person of colour shall be permitted to occupy any house in the town of Greenesborough, or in the town of Madison in the county of Morgan...

*1837*...if any White person or persons, are found playing and betting with Negroes, or playing or betting at any game with cards, for the purpose of betting upon, or winning or losing money, or any other thing or things, article or articles of value, or any property or any other article or articles, thing or things of value, may be indicted, and on conviction thereof, shall be imprisoned at hard labor in the Penitentiary...

... Whereas, free persons of color are liable to be taken and held fraudulently and illegally, in a state of slavery, by wicked white men...it shall and may be lawful for any Justice of the Inferior Court of any county of this State, upon the complaint of any free white person upon oath, showing that he has good reason to believe, and does believe that any person or persons of color are free, and are fraudulently and illegally held in slavery..., to arrest the person or persons so holding such person or persons of color in slavery...

*1840*...it shall and may be lawful for any free white citizen to file his petition in said Court, as in suits of a civil nature, against any person who may claim to exercise the rights and privileges of a free white citizen of this State, in which he shall distinctly allege that such...

...*person so claiming to exercise and enjoy the rights and privileges aforesaid is of mixed blood, and not a free white citizen; on the trial of any suit hereafter to be instituted by the authority of this act, it shall be lawful for the plaintiff to prove that the defendant is descended from, and stands in the third degree or generation to him or her who was or is not a free white citizen of this State, or of any other State whose Constitution and laws tolerate involuntary slavery, or that said defendant has one-eighth of Negro or African blood in his or her veins...*

1841...*An act to prohibit from sale or gift, all printed or written books, papers, pamphlets, writing paper, ink, and all other articles of stationery, of any kind whatsoever, to any slave or free person of color in this State...*

1849...*Any slave or free persons of color shall be put upon trial, for any offence against the laws of this State, that the said slave or free person of color has committed a capital offence, such slave or free person of color shall be immediately committed to the jail of the county wherein such offence was committed, if sufficiently secure...*

...*An act for the relief of all offenders against the late laws of this State prohibiting the introduction of slaves into the same for the purpose of sale, and prohibiting the sale, offer to sell, or the* purchase of slaves within a certain period after their introduction into this State; no person shall hereafter be convicted of any violation of the laws aforesaid, nor be held liable upon any bond for his appearance to answer to the charge of any such violation...

...it shall be the duty of each and all persons in this State taking up any runaway slave or slaves, when the owner or owners of the same is or are unknown, to deliver the same to the Jailor of the county where taken up within four days at least next after such taking up...

...An act to amend the several acts now in force regulating the fees of Magistrates and Constables in the State of Georgia... the fees of Magistrates and Constables in civil, criminal and cases of misdemeanor, shall be as follows: for whipping a slave or free person of color by sentence of Court of one dollar and thirty five cents...

*1850* ...An act to make it a penal offence for any conductor, fireman, engineer, or other officer or agent or managing or conducting any Railroad in this State to allow any slave to travel on the same, except under certain circumstances who shall allow any slave to enter and travel on the same, in the absence of the owner, overseer or employer of said slave, or without a written permit from the owner, overseer, or employer of said slave, shall be guilty of a high misdemeanor, and on conviction thereof in any court having jurisdiction of the same, shall be punished by imprisonment and labor in the Penitentiary for any time not less than one year nor longer than three years...

...Requires the Jailors of the several counties of this State to advertise and publish all runaway slaves in one of the papers of Milledgeville as they may direct or think proper...

*1851*...An Act, to protect the citizens of this State from danger, by the running at large of lunatic and insane slaves or free persons of color...

... upon the application of any person, under oath, setting forth that any insane or lunatic slave, or free person of color is running at large, and is a public nuisance, or dangerous to the public, the Justices of the Inferior Court of the county shall issue a warrant, directed to the Sheriff, Deputy Sheriff, or any Constable of said county, requiring him to bring such slave or free person of color before them...

*1855*... all owners, trustees, or agents of plantations, or farms in the county of Effingham, whereon there are three or more grown slaves employed, and where such owner, trustee or agent shall reside off and away from said plantation or farm, then it shall be the duty of such owner, trustee or agent, to keep employed and steadily residing on such plantation or farm, a white man for the purpose of controlling and disciplining said slaves...

*1856*...An act to compel owners of the slaves on plantations or farms in Effingham County to keep a white man on said farm or plantation.

...It shall be the duty of such owner, trustee or agent to keep employed and stately residing on such plantation or farm, a white man for the purpose of controlling and disciplining said slaves

*1859*...An Act to prevent free persons of color, commonly known as free negroes from being brought or coming into the state of Georgia.

...Any and all free persons of color who shall come or be brought into this State, shall on conviction of said violation be sold as a slave or slaves by the Sheriff of the County...

...Any free person of color wandering or strolling about, or leading an idle, immoral or profligate course of life, shall be deemed and considered a Vagrant, shall be punished by being sold into slavery, for any given time, in the discretion of the Judge of the Superior Court; the Judge shall pass an order requiring the Sheriff to advertise in some public Gazette of the State, the length of time for which such free person of color is to be *sold, also the place and time of sale; and the rules and regulations which now govern Sheriff sales of slaves...*

*...any words falsely and maliciously uttered, which impute to any free white woman of this State, carnal knowledge and connection with a slave, negro, or free person of color, shall he held, deemed and adjudged actionable, per se, and without allegation or proof of any special damage...*

*...the Recorder of said city (Augusta), in all cases of convictions before him of free persons of color or nominal slaves, for the violation of any of the ordinances of said city, shall have power to order said free person of color, to be sold into slavery, either for life or a term of years; which sale shall be made and perfected by the city Marshal, or his Deputy...*

*... the city Treasurer is hereby authorized to issue tax executions against all defaulting persons of color, for the amount of their taxes, or for a default to give in; which execution shall and may be levied upon said free person of color by said city Marshal or his deputy, and in like manner sold to pay said taxes, to shortest time bidder, who will pay the debt...*

*1863*...any slave, or free person of color, who shall go to the enemy, with the intention of giving them information of any kind, shall on conviction of the same, suffer such punishment as the Court trying said offence, may in its discretion inflict...

...any slave who shall leave the service of his owner or employer, and go over to the enemy, or shall leave the service of his owner or employer with the intention of going over to the enemy; or shall attempt to leave the service of his owner or employer for the purpose of going over to the enemy, shall, on conviction of the same, suffer such punishment as the Court trying said offence, may inflict in its discretion...

*1865*...free persons of color shall be competent witnesses in all the Courts of this State, in civil cases, whereto a free person of color is a party, and in all criminal cases wherein a free person of color is defendant, or wherein the offence charged is a crime or misdemeanor, against the person or property of a free person of color...

"The Black skin is not a badge of shame, but rather a glorious symbol of national greatness."

"God and Nature first made us what we are, and then out of our own created genius we make ourselves what we want to be. Follow always that great law. Let the sky and God be our limit and Eternity our measurement."

Marcus Garvey

# Revised Codes

...Any person may take up any negroes that shall be found out of the plantation or place where they belong, or incorporated town where they reside, acting unlawfully, or under suspicious circumstances, and if found with an offensive weapon shall take the same away, and if the negro is insolent, or refuses to answer, may whip said negro as the patrol may...

...No free person of color, non-resident of this state, shall be allowed at any time to come within the limits of this state...

...No free person of color, resident in this State, who shall sojourn for a period longer than six months in a non-slave holding state, shall be permitted to return to this state, and such person so returning shall be treated and dealt with as a non-resident free person of color...

...Every free person of color, over the age of sixteen years, resident in this State, shall on or by the first day of July next after the adoption of this Code, and all those under that age within one year after his or her arrival at said age, apply to the Ordinary of the county of his or her residence and demand to be registered as a free person of color...

...A free person of color, registered as aforesaid, by an absence of more than six months from this State, shall lose all the benefits of such *registration, and shall not be permitted again to have the benefit of this law...*

*...If any person shall give a ticket, pass or license to any slave who is the property, or under the care and control of another, without the consent of the owner, or other person having the care or control of such slave, such person offending shall be guilty of a misdemeanor...*

*...Any druggist, merchant, or other person who sell or furnish to any slave or free person of color, without the written permission of his master, employer, or guardian, any poisonous drug or medicine, shall be guilty of a high misdemeanor...*

*...Any person other than the owner, who sell or furnish to any slave or free person of color, any gun, pistol, bowie, knife, slung shot, sword cane, or other weapon used for the purpose of offence or defense, shall on indictment and conviction, be fined by the court in a sum not exceeding five hundred dollars, and imprisoned in the common jail of the county not exceeding six months...*

*...Any person who shall furnish any slave or free person of color, with any of the drugs enumerated in the preceding section (Sec.4513... arsenic, strychnine, hydrocyanic acid, and aconite,), or any other poisonous drug, shall be guilty of a felony...*

*...If a slave or free person of color is found by a jury to be an idiot or insane, and for that cause is discharged from prosecution for a capital offence, the presiding Judge shall pass such order for his future confinement as shall protect the community from his future acts...*

*...A slave shall never be punished for any offence not capital which was committed under coercion, order, threats or persuasion of his master or the person having control over him, if it shall clearly appear that the act was entirely the result of such influence, and not from any criminal intent...*

*...The confessions of a slave or free person of color, made to his master or guardian under the order of such master or guardian, shall not be held as voluntary confessions, or admitted in evidence as such, nor shall confessions made by a slave or free person of color, under punishment or the threat of punishment, be held admissible as evidence in any case...*

*...No slave shall be tried twice for the same offence, nor shall a slave be punished under a legal process for an offence not capital, when he has already received punishment by consent of the master and the person aggrieved by his act...*

*...The administering of poison to a free white person with intent to kill, shall constitute the offence specified in this article, although the poisoning failed of its effect from any cause...*

*...If a slave be convicted of voluntary manslaughter, either of a white person or of another negro, part of the punishment shall be branding in a conspicuous place with the letter "M"...*

*...Obedience and submission being the duty of a slave, much greater provocation is necessary to reduce a homicide of a white person by him to voluntary manslaughter, than is prescribed for white persons; in every case the question must be for the jury to decide whether the provocation was such as to justify uncontrollable passion in one accustomed to obedience and submission...*

*...Self defense is the right of every human being where his own life is unlawfully endangered. In the case of a slave, it must clearly appear that the act done was in defense of his master or family, is the only justification of a homicide by a slave...*

*...The punishment of a free person of color for immigrating into this State, in violation of its laws, shall be sale into perpetual bondage—to be had on conviction under the direction of the court—the proceeds to be paid into the Educational Fund of the county...*

# Guardianship Codes

**1810**...all free persons of color (native Indians excepted) who shall arrive in this state, shall within ten days after his or her arrival therein... shall register his or her name with the Clerk of the Superior court of the county in which he or she shall have arrived... and shall at the same time declare to the said Clerk his or her occupation or calling, the place of his or her residence and birth, the place from whence he or she shall last have come, the object for which he or she shall have come into this state, and the name of the person or persons in whose employment or service he or she may be engaged at the time of his or her arrival...

... the Judge of the Superior or the Justices of the Inferior Courts of the respective counties of this state, shall upon the written application of any free negro or person of color, made at any regular term of the said courts, praying that a white person resident of the county in which such application may be made, and in which such free person of color shall reside, may be appointed his or her guardian; and upon the consent in writing of such guardian, appoint such white person the guardian of such free person of color. And the said guardian of such free negro or person of color, shall be and is hereby vested with all the powers & authority of guardians...

*1829*... *guardians of free persons of color shall have the privilege, with the consent of the inferior courts, of resigning their appointments at any time they may wish to do so...*

*1833*...*each and every guardian of a free person of colour, shall, on or before the first day of May in each year, make a return in the clerk's office of the superior court of the county in which he lives, stating the name of such free person of colour, the date of his letters of guardianship, the occupation of his ward, and shall specify the means by which he obtained his or her freedom, and such return shall be sworn to by such guardian...*

*...it shall not be lawful for any person to give credit to any free person of colour, but on a written order of the guardian...*

*...Be it enacted ...That the negro slaves (called the public hands,) be sold and disposed of at the places and in the manner hereinafter pointed out and prescribed....And be it enacted ..That that portion of said negro slaves with the stock, utensils, and other public property connected with them, belonging to the eastern division, and attached to the Gainsville Station, be sold, one at a time, at public outcry, to the highest bidder...*

*1853*...it shall be the duty of the Inferior Courts of the several counties in this State to bind out to some fit and proper person all free negroes or other free persons of color between the ages of five and twenty-one years, upon its appearing to the Court, upon the evidence of two or more respectable persons, that such free negroes or persons of color are not being raised in a becoming and proper manner; and upon the person to whom said negroes or free persons of color are bound giving bond and sufficient security to said Court for their good treatment, and not to move them out of the limits of this State, and to discharge them from his or her service at the age of twenty-one years...

...if any person or persons to whom such negro or negroes or other free person of color is bound shall sell or cause to be sold into slavery such negro or free person of color, he, she or they shall be guilty of a misdemeanor...

*1866*...An Act to make valid contracts of apprenticeship made by citizens of Georgia with agents of the Freedmen's Bureau Whereas, The commissioner of the Freedmen's Bureau for this State has heretofore authorized the various agents of that bureau in all the counties of this State, to bind out to suitable persons minor colored persons of African descent, of both sexes, until they attain the age of twenty-one years...

# Revised Codes

...Guardians of free persons of color shall be appointed by the Ordinary at any regular term of his court, upon the written application of any such person of color residing in the county...

... The choice of the applicant, if over fourteen years of age, shall control the appointment; Provided, the written consent of such person to such appointment be filed, and the court is satisfied that such appointment is judicious for the ward and the public...

...Free persons of color under fourteen years of age shall be held and considered the wards of the guardian of their mother, until for good cause shown by any person, the Ordinary shall see proper to appoint another guardian for them, and such guardianship shall continue after their arrival at that age, until another is appointed for them...

...Guardians of free persons of color, as to the management of their persons or estates, are vested with all the powers and authority, and are subject to the same liabilities with guardians of minors...

...Credit shall not be given to any free person of color except upon the written order of the guardian, or unless subsequently ratified by him...

...Free persons of color, through their guardians, may acquire and hold real estate and personally (except slaves,) in this state. Any attempt directly or indirectly by trust or otherwise to secure the legal, equitable or any beneficial interest in slaves to a free person of color, shall be void, and the whole title to such slave shall be forfeited to the State...

...The Ordinary may, at his discretion, at any time, remove a guardian of a free person of color at the request of such free person of color, and may demand a bond and security for fidelity in the trust, either on appointment or at any subsequent time...

...Such guardians shall receive for their services the same compensation as guardians of minors...

"You can't separate peace from freedom because no one can be at peace unless he has his freedom."

Malcolm X

# Manumission

*1799...* That from and after the passing of this act the aforesaid James Stewart of the county of Burke, be, and he is hereby vested with and entitled to all the rights, privileges and immunities belonging to a free citizen of this state: Provided nevertheless, That nothing herein contained shall extend, or be construed to extend, to entitle the said James Stewart to serve in the capacity of a juror in any cause whatever, nor to render him a competent witness in any cause or case where the personal rights or property of any white person are or is concerned; nor to entitle the said James Stewart to vote at elections, nor to have or hold directly or indirectly, any office of trust or emolument, civil or military, within this state ...


...the following were manumitted in the year 1799...

...Judy Eltoft, of the county of Richmond...

...Lewis and China , property of James King, late of the city of Charleston ...

... Bridget, Leviny, Nancy, Daniel and Syrus , property of Ezekiel Hudnall...

...Harry M'Clendon, formerly the property of Jacob M'Clendon, and Rose his wife, formerly the property of Andrew M'Lean, have purchased their freedom, together with the freedom of their children Betsy and Kesiah, of and from their former owners, and have prayed that their freedom, as purchased, be secured by law...

*1801*...Lucy Barrot, and Betty Barrot, Jim, commonly called Jim Lary, late the property of John B. Lary...

...a mulatto girl named Nancy, late the property of Alexander Kevan...

...it shall not be lawful for any person or persons to manumit or set free any negro slave or slaves, negro, mulatto mustizo, or any other person or persons of colour, who may be deemed slaves at the time of this Act, in any other manner or form, than by an application to the Legislature for that purpose...

*1823*...Chloe, the property of James Robinson, late of Greene County...

*1831*...Sophia, now the property of Eli Fenn... in future the said Sophia shall be called and known by the name of Sophia Fenn...

*1834*...Sam, formerly the property of John Marler...

... Fanny Hickman, who is, and has been for more than thirty years, the wife of Paschal Hickman of the county of Burke, ...And whereas the said Paschal Hickman since his intermarriage with his said wife Fanny has had several children, and whereas by the laws of this State the said children follow the condition of their mother...

... John, Grove, Henry, William, Hetty, Eliza, and Frank, -- by and in consequence of said intermarriage between the said Paschal Hickman and Fanny his wife...

...Patsy and Cyrus, the wife and father of Solomon Humphries, a free person of colour; and Edmund, late the property of Theophilus Hill's estate, of Oglethorpe county...

*1855*...Boston, the property of E. B Way, Catharine P Wheeler, Thomas B. Wheeler, H R Wheeler and Eugene Bacon of the county of Liberty, and State aforesaid, and John Savage of the county of Chatham...

*1859*...from and after the passage of this act, any and every clause in any deed, will, or other *instrument made for the purpose of conferring freedom on slaves, directly or indirectly, within or without the State, to take effect after the death of the owner, shall be absolutely null and void...*

# Miscellaneous Codes

*1817*...A free person of color, over twenty years of age, may voluntarily sell him or her self into slavery. In all such cases the sale must be made openly at a regular term of the Inferior Court of the county, when the justices of said court shall privately examine such free persons of color to satisfy themselves of his or her free consent...

*1819*... Whereas, certain Africans illegally introduced into this state, were by the exertions of the collector of Brunswick, seized and delivered up to the state; and have been sold for the benefit of the same: BE it therefore enacted... That his Excellency the Governor shall be, and he is hereby authorized to pay to the said collector of Brunswick, out of the contingent fund, ten per centum on the amount of the proceeds of the sales of the said Africans...

*1824*...An act to apportion the representatives among the several counties in this state, according to the fifth enumeration, in conformity to the seventh section of the first article of the constitution. Whereas, the seventh section of the first article of the constitution directs that the House of Representatives shall be composed of members from all the counties according to their respective numbers of free white persons, including three-fifths of all the people of color...

*1838*...no gift of any Slave or Slaves hereafter to be made, shall be good or available in law or in equity against the creditors of the donor, or subsequent purchasers from him, without actual notice...

*1861*...An Act to authorize Elmira Mathews, a free person of color, to sell herself into perpetual slavery. ... The General Assembly do enact, That Elmira Mathews, a free person of color in Greene county, be, and she is hereby authorized to voluntarily become the slave of John        J.        Doherty        for        life.

*1919*...Whereas the losses sustained by the Southern States as a result of the war between the States were $4,000,000,000 value of emancipated slavery, $25,000,000 proceeds of captured and abandoned property of the South, and sixty-eight million dollars of taxes collected for cotton tax of 1867 and 1868....

# Revised Code

*...A free person of color, over twenty years of age, may voluntarily sell him or her self into slavery. In all such cases the sale must be made openly at a regular term of the Inferior Court of the county, when the justices of said court shall privately examine such free persons of color to satisfy themselves of his or her free consent...*

In the Cherokee language, the event is called
Nunna daul Isunyi—"the Trail Where They
Cried." The Cherokee Trail of Tears resulted
in the loss of thousands of lives under the
Indian Removal Act of 1830.

Tensions between Georgia and the Cherokee
Nation were brought to a crisis by the
discovery of gold near and around
Dahlonega, Georgia in 1829, resulting in the
Georgia Gold Rush, the first gold rush in U.S.
history. White gold speculators began
trespassing on Cherokee lands, and pressure
began to mount on the Georgia government
to fulfill the promises of the Compact of 1802.

# Native American Codes

*1835*...*From and after the first day of February next, it shall be unlawful for any Indian of the Creek nation to come within the limits of this state, excepting the city of Columbus; and whenever such Indian shall come within the limits of this state it shall be the duty of each and every civil and military officer in this state having knowledge or being informed of the fact, to arrest such Indian and lodge him in jail...*

*...If any Indian or descendant of an Indian, or white man the head of an Indian family, claiming the privileges of an Indian, shall employ any white man or slave belonging to a white man, or person of color other than the descendant of an Indian, as a tenant , cropper or assistant in agriculture, or as a miller or millwright, they shall for such offence, upon the same being established, by the testimony of two respectable witnesses, forfeit all right and title that they may have to any reservation or occupancy within the limits of this state...*

*1836*...*That the time prescribed in the said section of the above recited act, which limits the peaceable occupancy of the Cherokee Indians, and the privileges to which they are entitled by* law, in the lot or lots which they occupy under the provisions of the said act, be extended to the 25th day of May, 1838...

1837...An act to provide for the protection of the citizens of the Cherokee Country, and for the removal of Cherokee and Creek Indians from the limits of this State...

...there shall be organized in the counties of Union, Gilmer, Lumpkin, Murray, Walker, Floyd, Cass, Paulding, Cobb, Cherokee, and Forsyth, a company of sixty mounted men each, including officers, to be raised by volunteers where no, company is already organized and commissioned for that purpose...

... That the whole of said company shall be under the command of said Colonel and Lieutenant Colonel...

...That it shall be the duty of said commander to co-operate with the United States troops, if necessary, in removing all the Cherokee and Creek Indians from within the limits of this State, immediately after the twenty-fourth day of May next...

1838...that the wife and children of John Langley; the wife and children of Lock Langley;

the wife and children of David Shaw; Maliga Parris, his wife and children; the wife and children of Alfred Scudder; the wife and children of Alfred Hudson; the wife and children of John Rogers; William Rogers, wife and children; Robert Rogers, wife and children; Joseph Collins and children; Charles Vickory and children; the wife and children of Charles Harris; the wife and children of Bird Harris; the wife and children of William Harris; the wife and children of Parker Collins, deceased; Charlotte Vickory and children; the wife and children of Samuel Bennett; the wife and children of Silas Palmer; the wife and children of Lewis Blackburn; Charles Duncan, wife and children; George Welch and children; and George M. Waters and his descendants, be, and they, and each of them, are hereby permitted to enjoy all the rights and privileges that appertain and belong to the free citizens of this State; and that all disabilities heretofore imposed upon said persons of the Cherokee Tribe of Indians, be, and the same are hereby repealed.

*1845*...George Michael Lavender and Matthew Thompson, descendants of the Cherokee tribe of Indians, are hereby permitted to enjoy all the rights and privileges that appertain and belong to the free white citizens of this State...

...An act to grant the rights and privileges of citizenship to Isabella Hicks and her children,

87

*and Neely Justice, of the Cherokee tribe of Indians, and to remove all legal disabilities heretofore imposed on said tribe of Indians, so far as respects the said Isabella Hicks and her descendants, and the said Neely Justice...*

# Conclusion
## By Dan Moore, Sr.

*Seldom in American history were laws written against a group or race of people. However, explicit or implied there were laws written regarding Native Americans and Blacks, referred to as "coloreds" or "negroes."*

*As one turns the pages of law books it soon becomes abundantly clear that the "melting pot" was not all inclusive. So, the annals of history uncover a code of conduct that was designed to oppress, control and destroy certain people. Whether driven by fear, hatred or an inferiority complex, these laws, experienced, in many cases, swift passage and enactment. Most of these laws were at best inconsistent with the words penned in the founding documents of this nation.*

*"We the People" in the Constitution of The United States, obviously did not include nor embrace people whose land was being stolen nor other people of color brought here against their will whose free labor would build this "One Nation under God."*

*Today, as America travels thousands of miles from its borders under the pretence of creating a democracy in other lands, she must be ever mindful of her own past and present treatment of her laborers snatched from the shores of the world's greatest continent, Africa.*

*And so one can clearly conclude that "life liberty and the pursuit of happiness", "all men are* created equal" and "We the People" are mere phrases reflecting the rhetoric of the times, which is still too often alive in more subtle ways.

The founding fathers, so often held in high esteem, were framers of a democracy, riddled with hypocrisy which had no intention of including people of color.

For America to live up to the true meaning of its creed it must re-examine, repent and repair the damage and havoc it has wrought on its own citizens of color.

11191649R00060

Printed in Great Britain
by Amazon